This
David Bennett Book
belongs to

_____

_____

_____

_____

_____

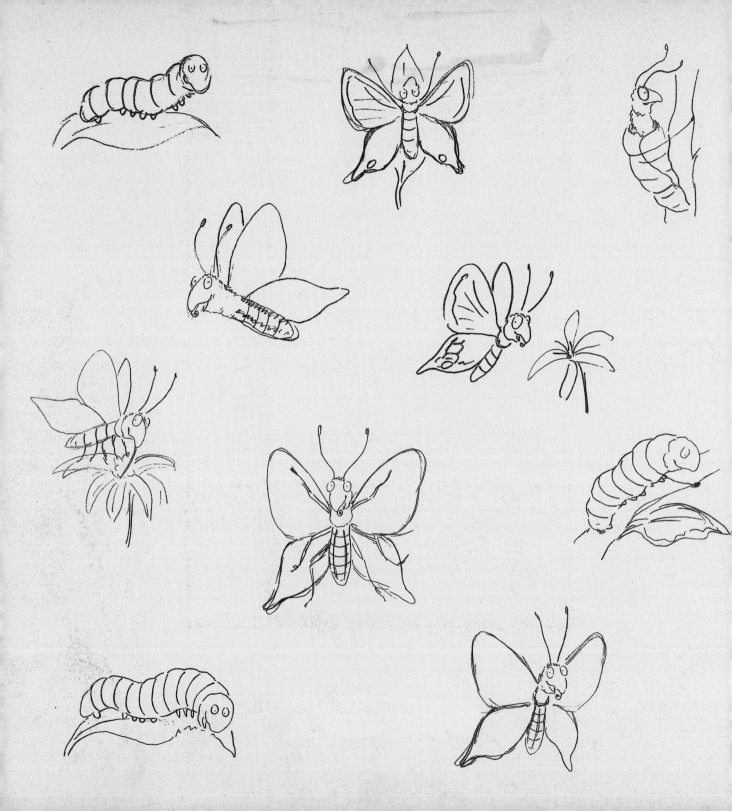

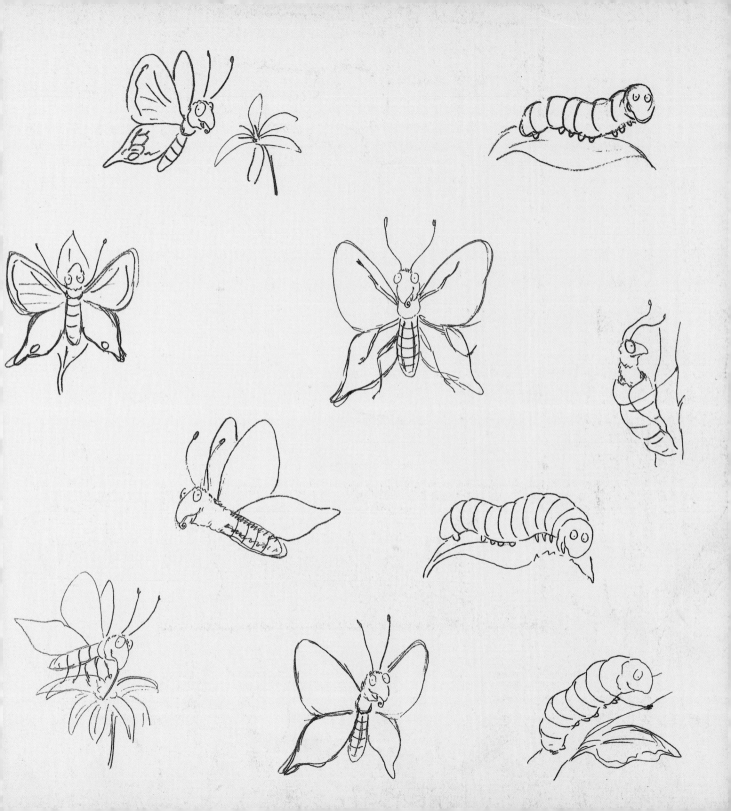

First published in paperback in 1993
by David Bennett Books Ltd,
94 Victoria Street, St Albans,
Herts, AL1 3TG.
First published in hardback in 1991
by Kingfisher Books

Consultant: Dr Julian Hector

BRITISH LIBRARY CATALOGUING IN PUBLICATION DATA
A catalogue record for this book is available
from the British Library.
ISBN 1 85602 052 5

Typesetting by Type City
Production by Imago
Printed in Hong Kong

I am a
Butterfly

Written by
Linda Bygrave

Illustrated by
Louise Voce

David Bennett Books

I am a butterfly.
I belong to a very large group
of little creatures called insects.

All insects have six legs.
Can you count mine?

I can fly because I have wings.
Compared with the size of my body
my wings are very big.

I have four wings.
They are much more colourful
on top than underneath.

My wings are covered in tiny pieces
called scales. Together, the scales
make up beautiful patterns.

Just look at the patterns
on some of my friends.

When I sit still, I hold my wings
above my back like this.
You can still see me.

It is hard to see some of my friends
because their wings look like
the plants they sit on.

I have two long stalks on my head
called antennae.
I use these to smell things.

I also have two large eyes,
one on each side of my head.
They are not like your eyes.

My mouth is not like yours either.
It is called a proboscis and it is
like a curled up straw.

Through my proboscis I can suck
the sweet food called nectar
from inside flowers.

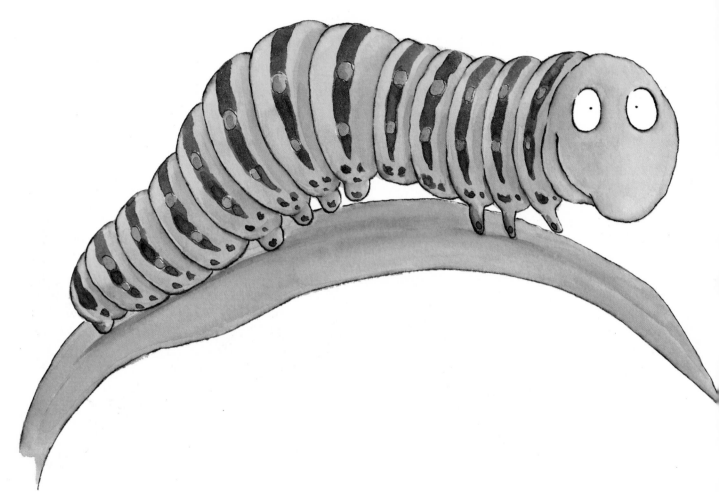

Did you know that a caterpillar
is a baby butterfly?
It's amazing, isn't it?

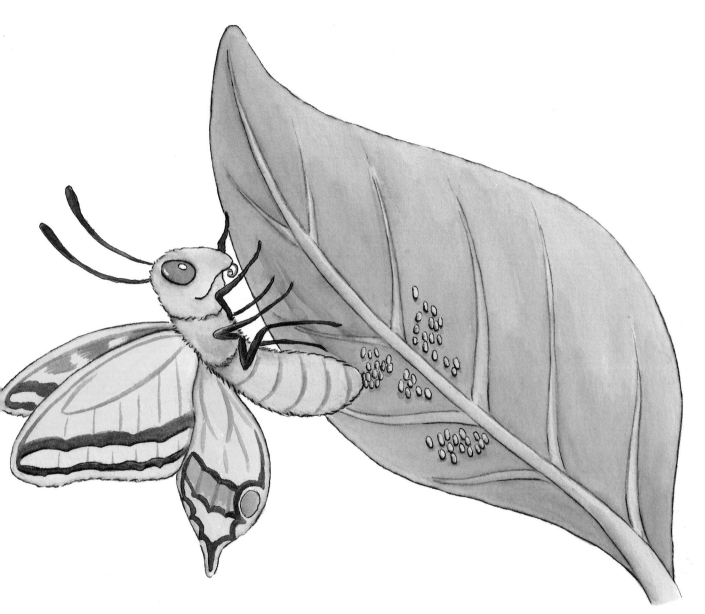

A mummy butterfly lays her eggs
on the underside of a leaf.
They are very, very tiny.

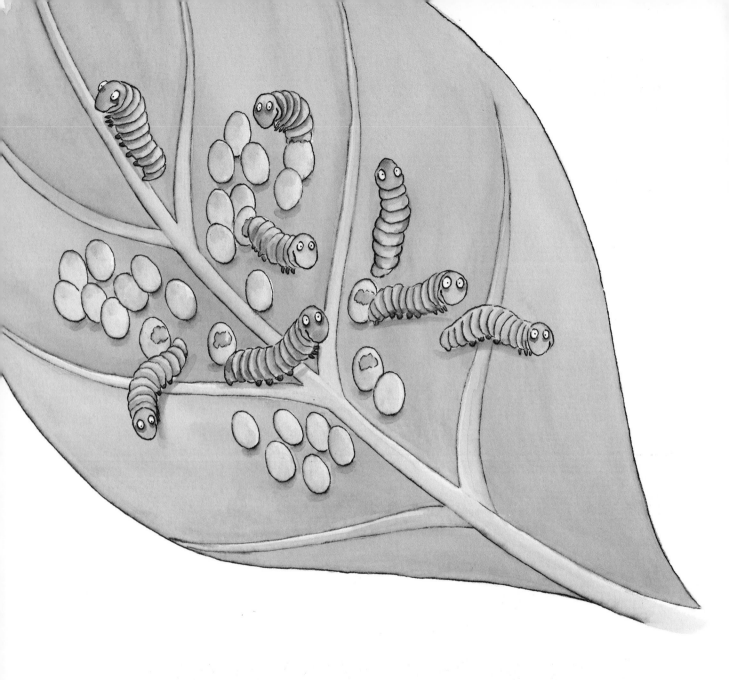

In a few days, the eggs hatch
and out come the caterpillars.

Caterpillars have very strong mouths.
They have special jaws
for munching leaves.

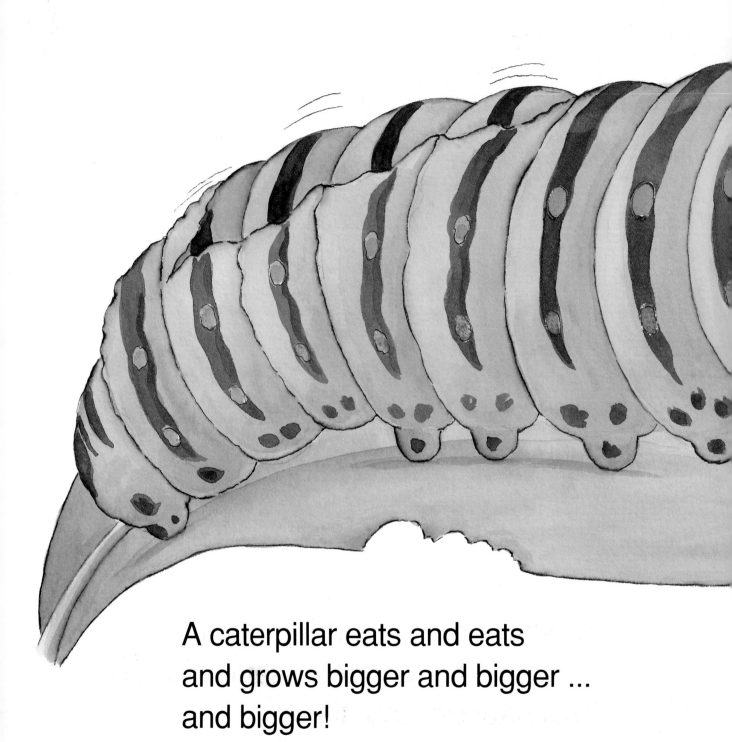

A caterpillar eats and eats
and grows bigger and bigger ...
and bigger!

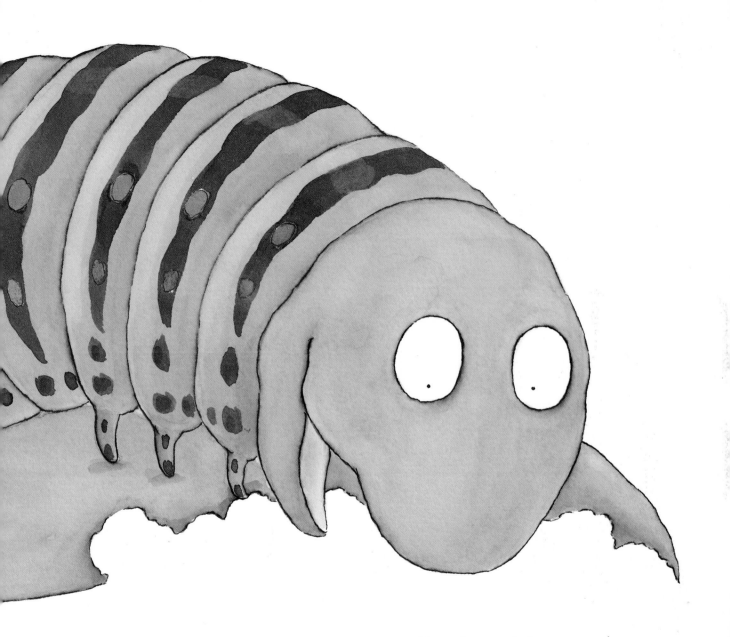

As it gets bigger, it splits its skin.
But it has a new one underneath.
This happens four times.

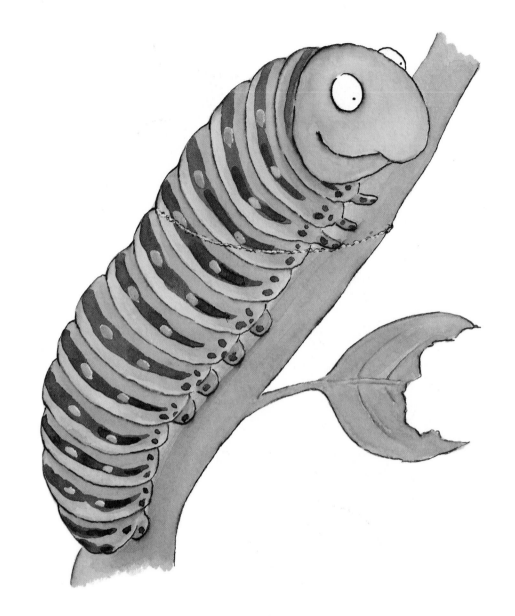

Soon the caterpillar is fully grown.
It holds on to the plant it has been eating
by its own silk thread.

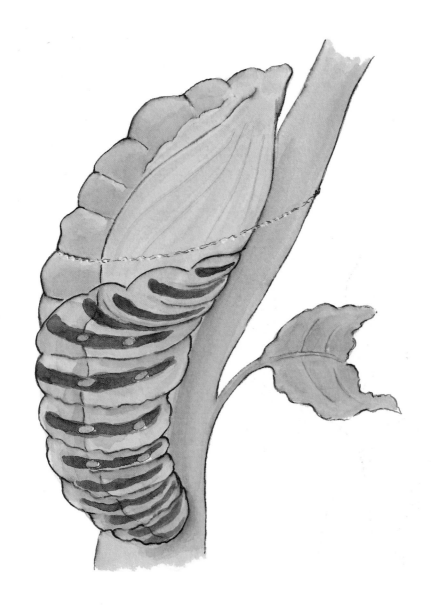

Now something very special happens.
Its skin splits and falls off.
Underneath you can see a pupa.

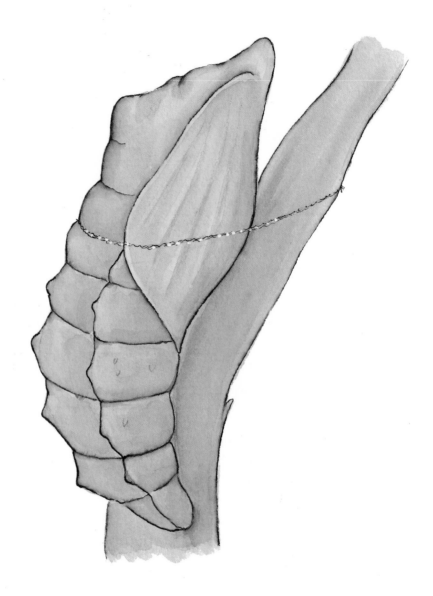

Inside the pupa, the caterpillar
doesn't eat or drink or move about.
It slowly changes into a butterfly.

This can take weeks or even months. When it is fully grown, the new butterfly comes out.

At first it is soft and crumpled.
After just a few hours, the butterfly
is strong and its wings are dry.

Now it is ready to fly.
I am that butterfly and it is time
for me to find some sweet nectar.
Goodbye!

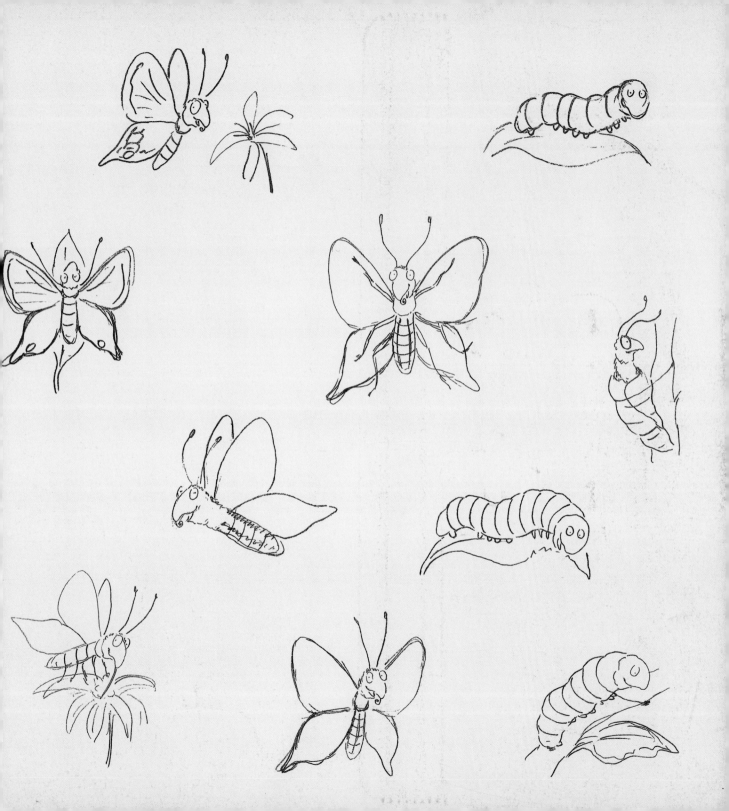

Other David Bennett paperbacks you will enjoy . . .